EARLY LIFE IN ANNASCAUL
1893 Tom Crean's family farm near Annascaul on the Dingle Peninsula, Kerry.
TOM, YOU LEFT THE GATE OPEN.
THE COWS WILL DESTROY THE SPUDS.
YOU'RE A WORTHLESS EEJIT.

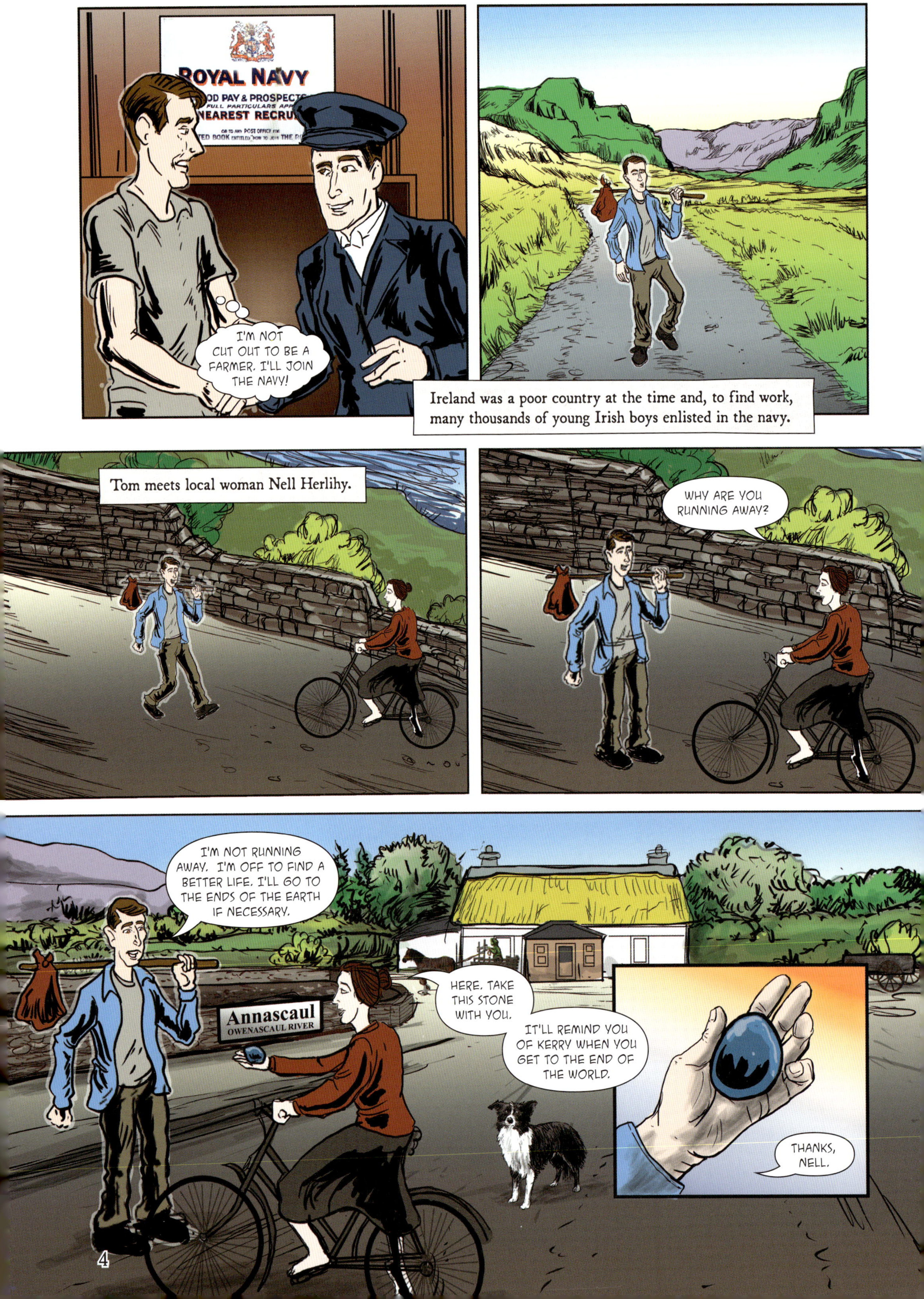
ROYAL NAVY
I'M NOT CUT OUT TO BE A FARMER. I'LL JOIN THE NAVY!
Ireland was a poor country at the time and, to find work, many thousands of young Irish boys enlisted in the navy.
Tom meets local woman Nell Herlihy.
WHY ARE YOU RUNNING AWAY?
I'M NOT RUNNING AWAY. I'M OFF TO FIND A BETTER LIFE. I'LL GO TO THE ENDS OF THE EARTH IF NECESSARY.
Annascaul
OWENASCAUL RIVER
HERE, TAKE THIS STONE WITH YOU.
IT'LL REMIND YOU OF KERRY WHEN YOU GET TO THE END OF THE WORLD.
THANKS, NELL.

# *DISCOVERY* EXPEDITION 1901–1904

The South Pole is 1,450 kilometres (900 miles) across unexplored ice fields, glaciers and mountains – a place where no one has gone before.
Antarctica is the coldest, windiest and driest place on earth. Winds of 320 km/h (200 mph) and temperatures of -40°C are common. It is a desert where neither rain nor snow ever falls.
South Georgia
South Atlantic Ocean
Elephant Island
Queen Maud Land
Weddell Sea
Ronne Ice Shelf
ANTARCTICA
Indian Ocean
SOUTH POLE
Ellsworth Land
Wilkes Land
Marie Byrd Land
Ross Ice Shelf
South Pacific Ocean
Ross Sea
Victoria Land
SOUTH POLE, HERE WE COME!
Tom is the first person to carry an Irish flag in Antarctica.
THIS IS HARDER THAN I EXPECTED.
I'M NOT SURE WE CAN KEEP THIS UP MUCH LONGER.
WILL WE FIND A BIG POLE WHEN WE GET THERE?
ALL WE'LL FIND IS ICE, ICE AND MORE ICE.

**November 1902** Captain Scott decides to send Tom and most other men back to the ship. He will continue towards the Pole with Irishman Ernest Shackleton and English doctor Edward Wilson.
SORRY, CREAN. YOU MUST GO BACK TO THE SHIP IN THE MORNING.
ROBERT SCOTT, EXPEDITION LEADER
ONE DAY, MAYBE, I'LL GET TO THE SOUTH POLE.
Tom walks south on his own for a few metres to achieve a 'furthest south' record.
I'LL MAKE MY OWN BIT OF HISTORY FIRST.
NO ONE HAS EVER STOOD THIS CLOSE TO THE POLE BEFORE. THEY CAN'T TAKE THAT AWAY FROM ME.
NOT BAD FOR A FARMER'S SON FROM KERRY.

Captain Scott, Shackleton and Wilson march south, but are forced to turn back 960 km (600 miles) from the South Pole.
*Discovery* is trapped by ice for two years. In desperation, they place dynamite to blast a path out of the Antarctic ice.
WE'LL NEVER ESCAPE IF THE DYNAMITE DOESN'T WORK.
BOOM
KABOOM
SMASHHH
BANG
I'M COMING BACK SOME DAY, AND I WANT YOU WITH ME NEXT TIME, CREAN.

*TERRA NOVA* EXPEDITION 1910–1913
**1910** Tom joins Scott's new expedition to conquer the South Pole. The ship is called *Terra Nova*, which means New Land.
Tom smuggles a pet rabbit in the snug bales of ponies' hay on *Terra Nova* and soon seventeen bunnies are born.
COME ON, TOM – LET'S HAVE ONE. YOU'VE GOT SEVENTEEN TO SPARE!
I HOPE MY FRIENDS CAN'T COUNT – I'VE PROMISED RABBITS TO TWENTY-TWO OF THE LADS SO FAR.

Terra Nova docks in Melbourne to pick up supplies and letters from home. Tom collects the mail.
THERE'S A SPECIAL TELEGRAM FOR YOU, SIR.
POST OFFICE TELEGRAM
Time handed in. Office of Origin and Service Instructions.
Am going South. Amundsen.
Scott learns that famous Norwegian explorer Roald Amundsen is racing him to the Pole.
THE NORWEGIANS ARE GREAT EXPLORERS, BUT I HOPE WE GET THERE FIRST.
Terra Nova departs from the port and heads to Antarctica.

Scott and his team set up base camp in preparation for the march to the Pole.
The explorers build provision depots in advance, because they cannot drag all the food and supplies needed for the long journey.
Scott takes hard-working ponies to pull sledges.
COME ON, BONES. WE'VE GOT WORK TO DO.
Tom, Lieutenant Henry Bowers and scientist Apsley Cherry-Garrard become trapped on drifting ice floes.
KILLER WHALES! WE'RE IN BIG TROUBLE.
WE'LL NEVER SAVE THE PONIES.
I'M GLAD I DIDN'T BRING BONES ON THIS TREK.
WATCH OUT. KILLER WHALES ARE BRUTAL.

Captain Scott is camped miles away, unaware of events.
I WONDER HOW CREAN AND THE PONIES ARE GETTING ALONG?
Tom volunteers to fetch help from Scott.
SAVE THE PONIES. I'LL GET CAPTAIN SCOTT.
THAT'S IMPOSSIBLE. HOW?
Tom hops from floe to floe with the killer whales circling menacingly.
DONE IT!
YOU'LL NOT BE HAVING ME FOR DINNER!

Tom's courage saves the lives of Lieutenant Bowers and Cherry-Garrard. However, the ponies are lost.
HANG ON! I'LL BE BACK.
Bowers and Cherry-Garrard's escape is celebrated at base camp. But officers and ordinary sailors are treated differently in the navy at this time.
THREE CHEERS FOR LIEUTENANT BOWERS AND MR CHERRY-GARRARD
YOUR BRAVERY SAVED THEM. THEY'D BE DEAD WITHOUT YOU, TOM.
I'M GOOD ENOUGH TO SAVE THEIR LIVES, BUT NOT GOOD ENOUGH TO EAT AT THE SAME TABLE.

1911 Captain Scott faces a dangerous journey of 1,450 km (900 miles) to the South Pole and 1,450 km (900 miles) back.
SOUTH POLE
POLAR PLATEAU
Amundsen Route
Captain Scott Route
Bay of Wales
Ross Ice Shelf
Cape Crozier
ROSS SEA
Elephant Island
Weddell Sea
ANTARCTICA
SOUTH POLE
Amundsen Route
Captain Scott Route
Ross Ice Shelf
Ross Sea
Will Amundsen's Norwegians win the race?
COME ON, BOYS! WE CAN DO IT!
TO THINK I STOOD HERE TEN YEARS AGO. ALL NEW GROUND FROM NOW ON. WONDER WHAT I'LL FIND ...
The ponies come to the end of their work. Their food has run out and it is necessary to put the animals out of their misery.
THANKS, OLD SON. YOU'VE BEEN A FAITHFUL SERVANT.

The South Pole lies beyond a high mountain pass and across hundreds of kilometres of ice.
I'M DRAINED!
ONLY ANOTHER 1,250 MILES TO GO, TAFF!
I CAN'T TAKE ANOTHER STEP. WHO'S COOK TONIGHT?
YOU ARE, TOM!

Hidden crevasses make the top of the mountain pass dangerous.

QUICK, GET ME OUT OF HERE!
SURE, IT'S YOUR BIRTHDAY TODAY AND THIS IS NO WAY TO CELEBRATE.
AND A VERY HAPPY BIRTHDAY, MY FRIEND.
!#@#!* ***
The two four-man sledging teams resume the trek south.

**January 1912** Scott's South Pole march is based on four-man units – food, tents, sledges, etc., are arranged for two four-man teams. At 240 km (150 miles) from the Pole, he changes his plans and adds an extra man to his team, meaning five will go south and three will return to base camp.

Edward Evans
Bill Lashly
Tom Crean
COUGH
COUGH
YOU'VE GOT A BAD COLD, CREAN.
EH?
I UNDERSTAND A HALF-SUNG SONG, SIR.
NO POLE FOR ME
Five go to the Pole; Tom, Bill Lashly and Lieutenant Teddy Evans must return.

**17 January 1912** Scott's party reach the South Pole and discover that Amundsen's Norwegians got there first. They are never seen alive again.

Tom, Bill Lashly and Lieutenant Evans face a dangerous journey of 1,200 km (750 miles) to reach safety. Evans is in charge.
Exhaustion and starvation are the biggest dangers. And it gets colder as the season changes from summer to autumn.
THAT'S IT, BOYS. WE MUST FIND THE DEPOT TOMORROW.
NOT MUCH OF A CHOICE – STARVE TO DEATH OR FREEZE TO DEATH
LIEUTENANT TEDDY EVANS, SCOTT'S NO 2
SEE ANYTHING?
YES – LOTS OF ICE!
WE'RE LOST!
IT MUST BE AT THE BOTTOM OF THE GLACIER. WE MUST GET DOWN FAST!
HOW DO WE GET DOWN QUICKLY?

WHOA!
AAAAAHHH!
WHHHOOOOSSSHHHH!
HANG ON, BOYS!
AAAAAAHHH!
In desperation, Tom, Bill Lashly and Lieutentant Evans jump aboard the sledge and toboggan down the icy slope.

Tom, Bill and Lieutenant Evans brush themselves down.
IS EVERYONE OK?
GOOD JOB WE HAD A SOFT LANDING.
LOOK – IT'S THE DEPOT!

The final 600 km (400 miles) of the journey is over a flat icefield called the Ross Ice Shelf. It is like being at sea and needs Evans to navigate.

I'M IN CHARGE. LEAVE ME BEHIND AND SAVE YOURSELVES. THAT'S AN ORDER!

DID HE SAY SOMETHING?
NAH, NEVER HEARD A WORD.

MUST BE THE WIND PLAYING TRICKS.

IS HE GONE?
I'LL SEE IF I CAN FEEL HIS BREATH.
THOUGHT WE'D LOST YOU FOR A MINUTE!

The trio are 56 km (35 miles) from base camp, but all the food has gone and Bill Lashly is also too weak to continue.
I'M THE LAST MAN STANDING. I'LL FETCH HELP.
DON'T GO, TOM. IT'S TOO DANGEROUS.
YOU'RE CRAZY. YOU HAVEN'T GOT A TENT OR ANYTHING TO EAT ...
YOU'VE ALREADY WALKED 1,500 MILES. HOW ARE YOU GOING TO DO ANOTHER 35 MILES ON AN EMPTY STOMACH?
I'VE GOT THREE BISCUITS AND TWO STICKS OF CHOCOLATE – SURE, THAT'S A FEAST!
I'LL BE BACK.

The area is treacherous and littered with dangerous crevasses.
Tom sits down to eat his biscuits and chocolate.
I'D PREFER A BIG JUICY STEAK AND A PILE OF SPUDS.
FOR EMERGENCIES. I MIGHT NEED A LAST BITE TO GET ME OVER THE LINE ...
... AND NELL'S LUCKY STONE.

NOTHING CAN SAVE ME FROM A BLIZZARD. I'D BETTER HURRY!
THUD
BANG
CRASSSHHHH
HELP ...
GET SOMETHING HOT INSIDE YOU.
I'VE GOT TO GO BACK OUT AND RESCUE BILL AND EVANS ...
YOU'RE GOING NOWHERE. I'LL FETCH THEM.
CRASSSHHHH

The blizzard rages for a day and a half before Dr Atkinson's team can rescue Lashly and Lieutenant Evans. Atkinson helps carry the two men into the hut, where they see Tom propped up in bed.
TOM, YOUR LONG LEGS SAVED US!
I WOULDN'T BE ALIVE WITHOUT YOU, TOM.
At base camp, the explorers wait months for Captain Scott to come back from the South Pole. Eventually, they realise the party must have perished.
Months later, the survivors go in search of the dead bodies.
THERE, THAT LOOKS LIKE A TENT.
IT MUST BE THEM.
GOODBYE, SIR.

IMPERIAL TRANS-ANTARCTIC EXPEDITION
At a special ceremony at Buckingham Palace, London, King George V awards Tom the Albert Medal, the highest award for gallantry.
1914 Tom cannot resist the call of the ice. Months after collecting his Albert Medal, he joins a new expedition to the Antarctic led by Kildare explorer, Sir Ernest Shackleton.

THIS IS GOING TO BE VERY HARD. BUT I WOULDN'T HAVE IT ANY OTHER WAY.
The Endurance expedition is the boldest and most dangerous ever made to the Antarctic. The aim is to walk 2,800 km (1,800 miles) coast to coast across the vast continent, a feat never done before.

At South Georgia, the last port before entering the ice, sailors from the whaling ships urge the explorers to abandon the expedition because of dangerous ice fields. Shackleton, Tom and *Endurance*'s captain, Frank 'Skipper' Worsley, consider the risks.
DON'T GO. IT'S TOO DANGEROUS. *ENDURANCE* WILL GET TRAPPED. SHE WILL BE CRUSHED!
Shackleton confers with his skipper, Frank Worsley, and Tom.
IT'S A BIG RISK.
IF WE DON'T GO NOW, WE'LL HAVE TO WAIT ANOTHER YEAR FOR WARMER WEATHER.
WE'VE COME TOO FAR TO TURN BACK.
ERNEST SHACKLETON, EXPEDITION LEADER
FRANK WORSLEY, *ENDURANCE* CAPTAIN
December 1914 *Endurance* ignores the warnings and leaves South Georgia. The ship is packed with food, supplies and sixty dogs.
OH THE WEARIN' OF THE GREEN, OH THE WEARIN' OF THE GREEN ...

January 1915 *Endurance*, with twenty-eight men on board, enters the icy waters of the Weddell Sea and is immediately trapped.
WE WILL BE HERE FOR MONTHS IF THE ICE DOESN'T BREAK UP.
WE'RE TRAPPED.
IT MIGHT NEVER LET GO.
FACE FACTS, LADS – WE'RE NOT GOING ANYWHERE.
ALL THAT MATTERS NOW IS TO GET OUT OF HERE ALIVE.
THIS IS THE END OF THE EXPEDITION – WE WON'T BE CROSSING THE LAND.
Although trapped and unable to sail, *Endurance* is carried for thousands of miles by the strong currents.

## *ENDURANCE* DOGS

*Endurance* is at the mercy of the ice and begins to topple over. The ship is doomed. Essential supplies and the dogs are taken onto the ice.
WE'LL MAKE DOG KENNELS ON THE ICE, LIKE IGLOOS.
I'LL GET THE SLEDGES READY.
LET'S CALL THEM DOGLOOS.
SHE'S GOING, LADS.
LOSING A SHIP IS THE WORST THING THAT CAN HAPPEN TO A SAILOR.
NO ONE KNOWS WE'RE HERE AND WE DON'T HAVE A RADIO TO CALL FOR HELP. NO ONE IS COMING TO RESCUE US
The nearest land is over 400 km (250 miles) across the broken ice.
IF WE CAN MAKE FIVE MILES A DAY, WE MIGHT MAKE OPEN SEA BEFORE THE FOOD RUNS OUT.
WE'LL BE LUCKY TO MAKE ONE MILE A DAY.

January 1916 Food is beginning to run out and there is no sign of the ice cracking open.
WE'LL CALL A HALT AND WAIT FOR THE ICE TO BREAK UP.
LET'S BUILD A CAMP AND CALL IT PATIENCE CAMP.
WE CAN MAKE ONE HOT DRINK A DAY.
EVERYONE WILL HAVE TO MAKE BIG SACRIFICES. EVEN THE DOGS
The dogs' food is almost gone and the animals will starve to death. No one wants them to suffer.
WE DON'T HAVE ENOUGH FOOD FOR OURSELVES.
WE DON'T HAVE A CHOICE.
WE HAVE TO PUT THE POOR ANIMALS OUT OF THEIR MISERY.
THIS IS THE HARDEST THING I'VE EVER DONE IN MY LIFE.

Food supplies are dangerously low and the men fear the worst.

Since entering the ice, the currents have carried the explorers around the Weddell Sea in a giant semicircle for over 3,000 km (2,000 miles).

April 1916 Open lanes of water can be seen in the ocean of ice.
The men prepare to launch the three lifeboats, called James Caird, Dudley Docker and Stancomb Wills.
HURRY UP, LADS. WE MUST BE READY FOR ANY OPENING.
TOM, YOU GO IN THE WILLS. SKIPPER WILL COMMAND THE DOCKER AND I'LL TAKE JAMES CAIRD.
IT'LL BE ROUGH OUT THERE AND WE'LL NEED ALL THE LUCK THAT'S GOING.
WHERE ARE WE GOING?
ELEPHANT ISLAND – IT'S ABOUT A HUNDRED MILES.
PUT YOUR BACKS INTO IT, LADS. WE MUST KEEP UP WITH THE OTHERS.
Tom takes control of Stancomb Wills, at just 6.3 metres (20 feet 8 inches) the smallest of the three boats. The Wills holds eight men, has a few oars and is weighed down by supply boxes.

*Stancomb Wills* is the slowest of the three vessels and soon falls behind.
WE'RE GETTING LEFT BEHIND. WE'VE GOT TO CATCH UP!
FASTER, LADS. WE'RE SINKING!

WHERE'S TOM?
HE MUST HAVE SUNK!
HAVEN'T SEEN HIM.
JAMES CAIRD
WE THOUGHT WE'D LOST YOU, OLD FRIEND.
YOU CAN'T GET RID OF ME THAT EASILY.
JAMES CAIRD
THANKS BE TO HEAVEN!
I KNEW YOU'D WAIT.
THEY MAKE 'EM TOUGH IN KERRY.

The three boats tie up alongside an ice floe and the men try to snatch some sleep. But the floe suddenly breaks apart.
HELP, HELP!
GOTCHA!
I DON'T HAVE ANY SPARE CLOTHES. I'LL FREEZE TO DEATH.
NONE OF US HAS GOT ANY SPARE.
WAIT A MINUTE ...
RUNNING WATER DOESN'T FREEZE. HE WON'T TURN INTO A BLOCK OF ICE IF HE KEEPS MOVING.

The boats approach Elephant Island in very rough seas.
THERE'S ELEPHANT ISLAND. COME ON, BOYS. ONE LAST HEAVE – YOU CAN DO IT!
DRY LAND AT LAST!
STEADY!
Tom steers the *Wills* through rocky reefs.
CAREFUL ... DON'T HIT THE ROCKS!

*Wills* is first on the beach as the explorers reach dry land for the first time in almost 500 days – one year and five months.
WE'VE MADE IT!
THE GLACIER WILL GIVE US ALL THE FRESH WATER WE CAN DRINK.
WE NEED A HOT DRINK – QUICKLY.
NO ONE'S COMING TO GET US. SHIPS DON'T COME THIS WAY.
WE DON'T HAVE A RADIO TO CALL FOR HELP ANYWAY.
WE'RE ON OUR OWN.

The nearest land to Elephant Island where they might find a ship is South Georgia – about 1,300 km (800 miles) across the roughest ocean on earth.
Many of the twenty-eight explorers are struggling and will not survive the voyage to South Georgia.
I'LL TAKE SIX IN THE *CAIRD* AND FIND A BOAT AT SOUTH GEORGIA.
SKIPPER WILL COMMAND THE *CAIRD*. TOM, I WANT YOU TO STAY HERE TO LOOK AFTER THE MEN.
I'M A SAILOR – I WANT TO TAKE MY CHANCES WITH THE SEA. DON'T LEAVE ME HERE.
I'LL NEED THE BEST SAILORS FOR THIS TRIP ... OK YOU'RE IN!
*James Caird* is the only hope for the twenty-two castaways on Elephant Island. If the *Caird* is lost on the stormy seas, they will all die.

THE *JAMES CAIRD* VOYAGE
GOOD LUCK, LADS!
HURRY BACK!
DO YOU KNOW WHAT DAY IT IS?
IT'S THE TWENTY-FOURTH OF APRIL - EASTER MONDAY - 1916.
I WONDER WHAT'S HAPPENING AT HOME IN IRELAND.

Crossing the Southern Ocean on the long voyage to South Georgia means navigating storms, hurricanes touching 120 km/h (80 mph), 15-metre (50-foot) waves and the freezing cold.
OH THE WEARIN' OF THE GREEN, OH THE WEARIN' OF THE GREEN ...
NOTHING WORRIES TOM.
OH THE WEARIN' OF THE GREEN ...

Layers of sea spray freeze on the vessel during the bitterly cold night and threaten to capsize the *James Caird*.
WE'LL OVERTURN IF WE DON'T CHIP THE ICE AWAY.
SOMEONE WILL HAVE TO CRAWL OUT AND SMASH THE ICE OFF.
LEAVE IT TO ME.
CAREFUL, TOM. DON'T GET TOSSED OVERBOARD.
LET'S ALL TAKE A TURN OUT THERE.

Another big threat to the *James Caird* comes in the middle of the night when Tom spots a white light on the horizon.
WHAT'S THAT LIGHT ON THE HORIZON? IT CAN'T BE DAWN YET.
THAT'S A HUGE WAVE!
HOLD ON, HOLD ON FOR YOUR LIVES!
I'VE NEVER SEEN A WAVE THIS BIG!
CRASSHH!!
BAIL LIKE YOU'VE NEVER BAILED BEFORE!
SPLASSSH
WHUMMP
SLOSSHH

After more than two weeks at sea, the men are overjoyed to see birds flying overhead, a sure sign of land ahead.
LAND! LAND AHOY!

Powerful storms and 120 km/h (80 mph) winds strike *James Caird* as the vessel comes close to South Georgia.
IT'S TOO DANGEROUS. WE'LL BE SMASHED AGAINST THE ROCKS IF WE GET ANY NEARER.
WE'LL HAVE TO SPEND ANOTHER NIGHT AT SEA IN THIS HURRICANE.
SURVIVING IS ALL THAT MATTERS. EVEN IF WE HAVE TO STAY AT SEA.
WE WON'T SURVIVE ANOTHER NIGHT IN THESE SEAS.
IT'S NOW OR NEVER.
THERE – THAT BEACH WILL HAVE TO DO.
IT'S OUR LAST HOPE.

After navigating rocky reefs, the *James Caird* crashes onto the stony beach.
THE LAST TIME WE WERE HERE ON SOUTH GEORGIA, WE HAD A FULLY STOCKED SHIP AND ALL THE SUPPLIES IN THE WORLD.
ALL WE'VE GOT NOW IS THE CLOTHES WE'RE WEARING.
YOU'RE GOING NOWHERE, MY LAD.

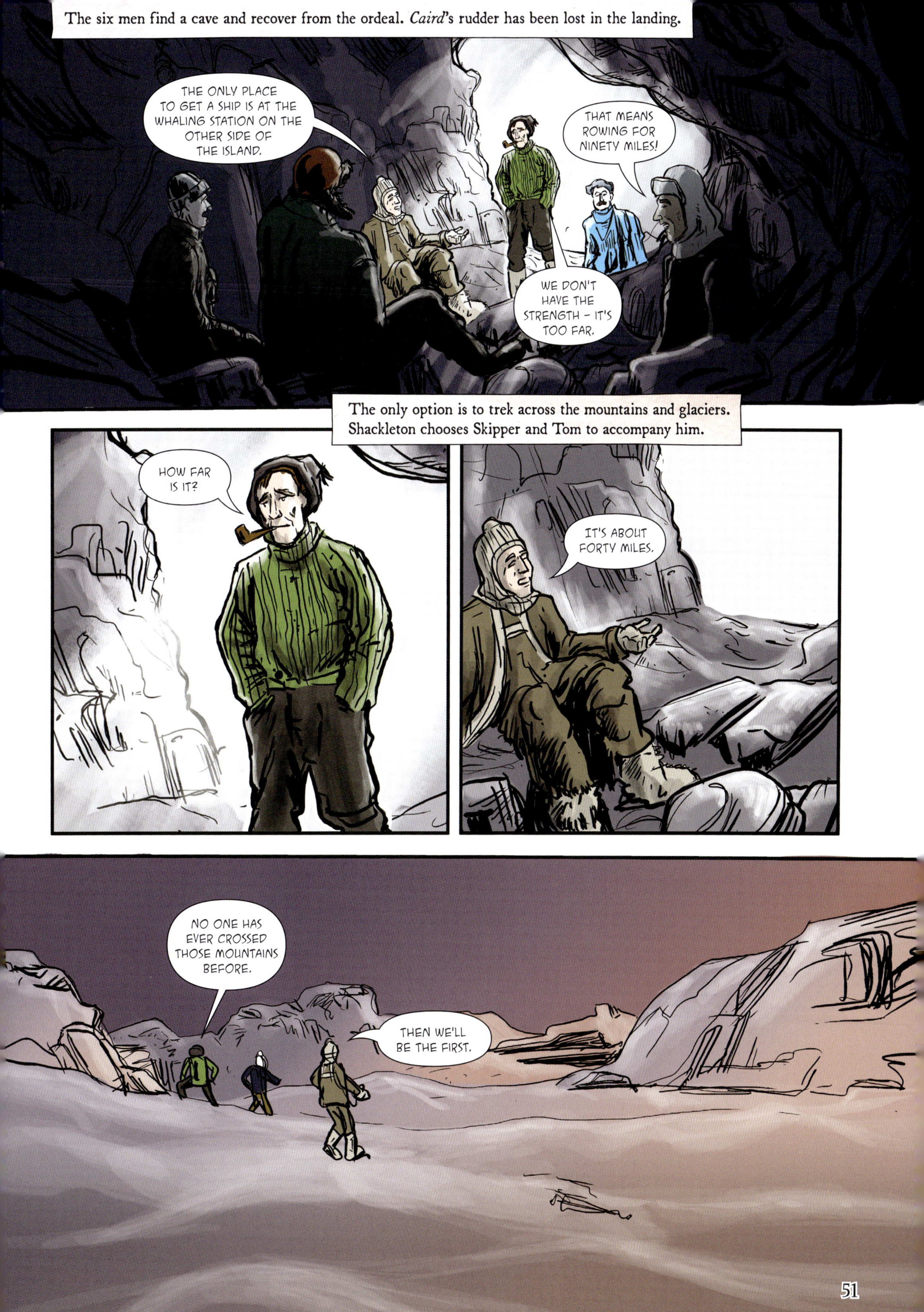
The six men find a cave and recover from the ordeal. *Caird*'s rudder has been lost in the landing.
THE ONLY PLACE TO GET A SHIP IS AT THE WHALING STATION ON THE OTHER SIDE OF THE ISLAND.
THAT MEANS ROWING FOR NINETY MILES!
WE DON'T HAVE THE STRENGTH – IT'S TOO FAR.
The only option is to trek across the mountains and glaciers. Shackleton chooses Skipper and Tom to accompany him.
HOW FAR IS IT?
IT'S ABOUT FORTY MILES.
NO ONE HAS EVER CROSSED THOSE MOUNTAINS BEFORE.
THEN WE'LL BE THE FIRST.

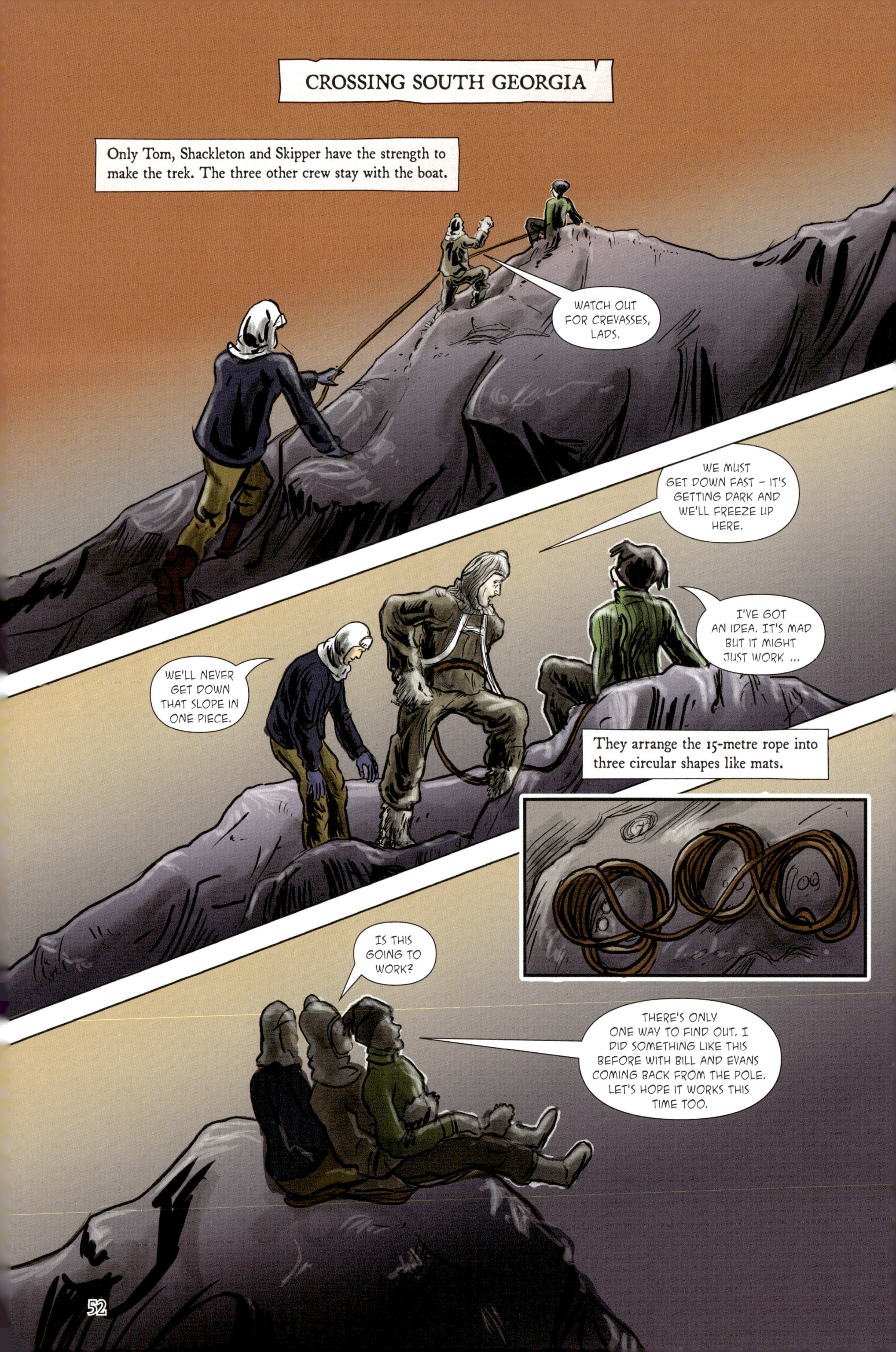
CROSSING SOUTH GEORGIA
Only Tom, Shackleton and Skipper have the strength to make the trek. The three other crew stay with the boat.
WATCH OUT FOR CREVASSES, LADS.
WE MUST GET DOWN FAST – IT'S GETTING DARK AND WE'LL FREEZE UP HERE.
I'VE GOT AN IDEA. IT'S MAD BUT IT MIGHT JUST WORK ...
WE'LL NEVER GET DOWN THAT SLOPE IN ONE PIECE.
They arrange the 15-metre rope into three circular shapes like mats.
IS THIS GOING TO WORK?
THERE'S ONLY ONE WAY TO FIND OUT. I DID SOMETHING LIKE THIS BEFORE WITH BILL AND EVANS COMING BACK FROM THE POLE. LET'S HOPE IT WORKS THIS TIME TOO.

Tom, Shackleton and Skipper cling to each other as they hurtle down the icy slope.
WHOOOOOOAAA
MY TROUSERS ARE RIPPED! WHAT HAPPENS IF THERE ARE WOMEN AT THE WHALING STATION?
I DON'T THINK THE GIRLS WILL BE CHASING ANY OF US – WE HAVEN'T HAD A WASH FOR A YEAR AND A HALF!

Tom, Shackleton and Skipper crowd around the stove for their last scrap of food.

IT CAN'T BE TOO FAR TO THE WHALING STATION NOW.
IT SHOULD BE AT THE END OF THIS STREAM.
STOP - IT'S A SHEER DROP!
OH NO - WE'LL HAVE TO GO BACK.
NO. WE'LL CLIMB DOWN. A COLD SHOWER WILL DO US ALL GOOD.
I'LL GO FIRST.
YOU DEFINITELY NEED A SHOWER, TOM!
COME ON DOWN!. IT'S LOVELY.

ONLY A FEW MORE STEPS ...
GHOSTS, THEY'RE GHOSTS! RUN!
WHO ARE YOU?
MY NAME IS SHACKLETON. THESE ARE TOM CREAN AND SKIPPER WORSLEY.
WE ALL THOUGHT YOU WERE LOST AT SEA!
These are the first words they have spoken to another person for almost a year and a half.

Tom, Shackleton and Skipper spend over four months desperately trying to get back to Elephant Island. They borrow three different ships, but are unable to break through the thick ice.

**23–30 May** *Southern Sky* (whaler) blocked by ice.

**10–16 June** *Instituto da Pesca No 1* (Uruguayan fishing vessel) not equipped for icy seas.

**12 July – 8 August** *Emma* (wooden schooner) too frail.

At the fourth attempt, they borrow a small ship from the Chilean navy called *Yelcho*, which breaks through the ice on **30 August 1916**.

RESCUE
Tom's last act as an explorer is to rescue the castaways on Elephant Island.
Tom, Shackleton, Skipper and twenty-two castaways return to Chile to celebrate the rescue.

Tom returns home and rejoins the navy, which is at war with Germany.

1917 Tom takes leave from the navy and marries Nell Herlihy.
I'LL BE BACK WHEN THIS WAR FINISHES. MY EXPLORING DAYS ARE OVER.
I'M GOING TO OPEN A PUB HERE IN ANNASCAUL.
PEOPLE WILL FLOCK TO SEE THE FAMOUS EXPLORER, TOM CREAN.
1920 Tom leaves the navy after twenty-seven years' service and settles in Annascaul with Nell. They have three children.

1920 Fighting in the War of Independence grows worse as Tom begins to build his new life.
THE WAR OF INDEPENDENCE
100 POLICE BARRACKS BURNED
THE WAR OF INDEPENDENCE
100 POLICE BARRACKS BURNED
Tom's oldest brother, Con Crean, a sergeant in the Royal Irish Constabulary, is ambushed by the IRA on a country lane in west Cork.
UPTON
TRAIN STATION
YE WERE WARNED NOT TO SERVE THE CROWN!
ANYONE WEARING A BRITISH UNIFORM WILL GET THE SAME!

THE SOUTH POLE INN
INN BARR'S
I NEVER THOUGHT IRISHMEN WOULD SHOOT EACH OTHER.
YOU'RE IN DANGER TOO. ALL YOUR YEARS IN NAVY UNIFORM MAKES YOU A TARGET. BE CAREFUL.
I MUST FIND A WAY TO PROTECT YOU AND OUR GIRLS.
HOW?
WITH SILENCE ...
Tom prepares to put his past exploits behind him and places his Polar Medals in a wooden box for safekeeping.
I'LL NEVER SAY A WORD TO A SOUL ABOUT THE ICE.
I WON'T NEED MY LUCKY STONE ANY MORE. I'M NEVER LEAVING KERRY AGAIN!

1921 Tom receives a telegram.
Dan Foley's Bar Annascaul
WHO'S IT FROM?
SHACKLETON. HERE, TAKE A LOOK.
HE WANTS YOU TO GO BACK TO THE ICE WITH HIM. YOU PROMISED YOU'D NEVER GO AGAIN.
POST OFFICE TELEGRAM
I am going back South Shackleton
MY EXPLORING DAYS ARE OVER – I'VE GOT A LONG-HAIRED PAL NOW.
POST OFFICE

Tom keeps his word and never speaks to a soul about his adventures.
1927 Tom opens his pub and calls it the South Pole Inn. It is still open.
1938 Tom Crean dies at the age of sixty-one and takes his astonishing story to the grave.
Tom is buried in the cemetery in Ballynacourty, near Annascaul. A nearby stream runs down the hill past the South Pole Inn.
CREAN
His gravestone bears the quotation:
Home is the Sailor,
Home from the Sea.

First published 2025 by
The O'Brien Press Ltd,
12 Terenure Road East, Rathgar,
Dublin 6, D06 HD27, Ireland.
Tel: +353 1 4923333; Fax: +353 1 4922777
E-mail: books@obrien.ie
Website: obrien.ie
The O'Brien Press is a member of Publishing Ireland.

ISBN: 978-1-78849-455-7


Lettering by Louise McSharry
Cover design by Emma Byrne



2 4 6 7 5 3 1
26 28 27 25

Printed and bound by Drukarnia Skleniarz, Poland.
The paper in this book is produced using pulp from managed forests.

Published in
DUBLIN
UNESCO
City of Literature

Great Irish books
O'BRIEN
obrien.ie

# TOM CREAN
# IRISH ANTARCTIC HERO

MICHAEL SMITH DAVID BUTLER

LETTERING BY LOUISE McSHARRY

THE O'BRIEN PRESS
DUBLIN

## Dedications

**In memory of Mary and Eileen Crean (Tom Crean's daughters), Tom Kennedy (proprietor of The South Pole Inn) and Margaret Walshe (Shackleton Museum Athy)**

For Barbara, Daniel, Nathan, Lucy and Zoe
*Michael Smith*

For Marcella, Erin, Ava and Kian, my parents John and Mary
*David Butler*

Michael Smith is author of *An Unsung Hero*, the classic biography of Tom Crean, and *Iceman: Tom Crean*, for younger readers. Michael, a Polar historian, rescued Crean from obscurity and brought his story onto the curriculum in Irish schools. Michael's books have assisted with the development of films and documentaries and have been translated into other languages, including Irish, German, Spanish and Chinese. His books include: *Icebound in the Arctic: The Mystery of Captain Francis Crozier and the Franklin Expedition, Shackleton: By Endurance We Conquer* and *Great Endeavour: Ireland's Antarctic Explorers*. Michael was an award-winning journalist with *The Guardian* and *The Observer*.
Website: micksmith.co.uk

Originally from Kildare, animator and illustrator David Butler now lives in Portarlington, County Laois. He is a graduate of the Dun Laoghaire Film Institute of Ireland, Animation Production course. He has worked on several award-winning projects, including the BAFTA award-winning *Sir Gawain and the Green Knight*. David has illustrated four original children's books with Mario Corrigan and the graphic novel *Michael Collins: Ireland's Rebel Son*. With author Gavin McCummiskey, David also illustrated the graphic novel *Shackleton: The Voyage of the James Caird*.
Website: anithing.ie • Instagram: @anithingartist • Twitter: @anithingartist

Louise McSharry is a graphic designer and illustrator from Laois. With a passion for bold aesthetics and a deep understanding of the power of brand identity, Louise has carved her niche in graphic branding, book design and logo development. Louise approaches visual design with a unique blend of colourful, artistic flair and professional expertise to elevate projects.
Website: 2funkidesign.com